Pebble®
Plus

he

it

my

What Is a
PRONOUN?

we

their

you

by Sheri Doyle

Consulting Editor: Gail Saunders-Smith, PhD

PARTS
OF
SPEECH

CAPSTONE PRESS
a capstone imprint

Pebble Plus is published by Capstone Press,
1710 Roe Crest Drive, North Mankato, Minnesota 56003.
www.capstonepub.com

Library of Congress Cataloging-in-Publication Data
Doyle, Sheri.
  What is a pronoun? / by Sheri Doyle.
      p. cm. — (Pebble plus. Parts of speech.)
  Includes index.
  Summary: "Full-color photographs and simple text provide a brief introduction to pronouns as parts of speech"—Provided by publisher.
  ISBN 978-1-62065-127-8 (library binding)
  ISBN 978-1-4765-1736-0 (ebook PDF)
1. English language—Pronoun—Juvenile literature. 2. English language—Parts of speech—Juvenile literature. 3. English language—Grammar—Juvenile literature. I. Title.

PE1261.D69 2013
425'.55—dc23   2012031638

Editorial Credits
Jill Kalz, editor; Heidi Thompson, designer; Marcie Spence, media researcher; Laura Manthe, production specialist

Photo Credits
Alamy Images: Gordon M. Grant, 9; Capstone Studio: Karon Dubke, 21; iStockphoto: Dean Mitchell, 11; Shutterstock: Alena Ozerova, 13, Bernd Schmidt, 7, bikeriderlondon, 19, Blaj Gabriel, cover (boy in red), Blend Images, (gymnast), John Kropewnicki, 15, oliveromg, 5, Regien Paassen, 17, Rob Marmion, cover (girl and boy), Subbotina Anna, cover (dragonfly)

Note to Parents and Teachers

The Parts of Speech set supports English language arts standards related to grammar. This book describes and illustrates pronouns. The images support early readers in understanding the text. The repetition of words and phrases helps early readers learn new words. This book also introduces early readers to subject-specific vocabulary words, which are defined in the Glossary section. Early readers may need assistance to read some words and to use the Table of Contents, Glossary, Read More, Internet Sites, and Index sections of the book.

Printed in the United States of America in North Mankato, Minnesota.
092012   006933CGS13

Table of Contents

Hello, Pronoun!

Do *you* know what *it* is?
A pronoun! A pronoun is
one part of speech. It takes
the place of a noun.

me

you

her

him

it

A pronoun can make

a sentence shorter.

When a pronoun is used,

the noun is not repeated.

After the polar bear eats, the polar bear naps.

After the polar bear eats, _it_ naps.

One or Many

Singular pronouns stand for one person or object. One girl is "she." One donut is "it." Here are more: I, me, you, he, her, him.

I pet the pig. You can pet it with me.

9

Plural pronouns stand for more than one person or object. They are "we," "us," "they," and "them." "You" can stand for one *or* many.

The geese honk at <u>us</u>.

<u>They</u> are hungry!

<u>We</u> feed <u>them</u>.

<u>You</u> can too!

It's Mine! It's Ours!

Singular possessive pronouns show ownership by one person or object. "My," "her," and "his" are examples. So are these: mine, your, yours, hers, its.

I have a cat. <u>My</u> cat has long hair.

You have a cat. <u>Your</u> cat has short hair.

Plural possessive pronouns show ownership by more than one person or object. Here they are: our, ours, your, yours, their, theirs.

Our boat is faster than their boat.

More Pronouns

Sometimes a pronoun stands
for any, some, or every person
or object. "Anybody," "anyone,"
and "something" are examples.

Everything on the table looks yummy.

Anyone can take a treat.

17

Reflexive pronouns end
in "self" or "selves."
They refer back to the
subject of the sentence.

I see <u>myself</u> in the mirror.
subject

We see <u>ourselves</u> in the mirror.
subject

Anything and *everyone*

can be pronouns.

You have probably played

with many of *them* today.

Glossary

noun—a word that names a person, place, or object

object—anything that can be seen or touched; a thing

plural—more than one

possessive—showing ownership or belonging

reflexive—referring or turning back to oneself

repeated—said or done again

singular—of or having to do with one person or object

subject—a word or group of words in a sentence that tells whom or what the sentence is about

Read More

Ganeri, Anita. *Naming Words: Nouns and Pronouns.* Getting to Grips with Grammar. Chicago: Heinemann Library, 2012.

Heinrichs, Ann. *Pronouns.* Mankato, Minn.: The Child's World, 2011.

Loewen, Nancy. *If You Were a Pronoun.* Word Fun. Minneapolis: Picture Window Books, 2007.

Internet Sites

FactHound offers a safe, fun way to find Internet sites related to this book. All of the sites on FactHound have been researched by our staff.

Here's all you do:

Visit *www.facthound.com*

Type in this code: 9781620651278

Super-cool stuff! Check out projects, games and lots more at **www.capstonekids.com**

Index

Word Count: 182

Grade: 2

Early-Intervention Level: 22